Elliott Carter

Poems of Louis Zukofsky

Soprano Part

for Soprano and Clarinet in B-flat

Archive Edition

HENDON MUSIC

BOOSEY & HAWKES

AN IMAGEM COMPANY

DISTRIBUTED BY

HAL•LEONARD® CORPORATION

7777 W. BLUEMOUND RD. P.O. BOX 13819 MILWAUKEE, WI 53213

www.boosey.com
www.halleonard.com

Commissioned by The Jerusalem International Chamber Music Festival,
the Nash Concert Society for the Nash Ensemble,
and the Tanglewood Music Center
with support from the Paul Jacobs Memorial Fund.

PERFORMANCE NOTE

The two performers should be balanced dynamically,
so that the clarinet always remains under the voice.

PROGRAM NOTE

As an admirer of Louis Zukofsky's poetry, I have often thought of setting it to music.
This was encouraged by recently finding out that Ezra Pound was very impressed by it.
So I chose nine short poems and set them for voice and clarinet, the last of which
refers to his son Paul, the eminent violinist.

—Elliott Carter

Text is from: *Complete Short Poetry*
by Louis Zukofsky

for Paul

POEMS of LOUIS ZUKOFSKY
for Clarinet and Soprano

1. Tall and Singularly Dark

Louis Zukofsky

Elliott Carter

Printed 14 December 2009

For noth-ing but the sun_ is there and peace vi - tal with the

sun,_____ The heav - i - est_ chang - es shift_ through_____ no fea - ture more than a

smile,_____ Cur - rents spread,_ and are gone,___ and

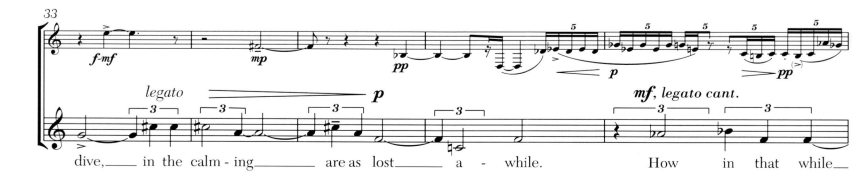

as the high___ waves ap - - - pear,_____ you_____

dive,___ in the calm - ing_____ are as lost_____ a - while. How in that while_____

Nov. 11, 2008 NYC

2. Alba (1952)

Louis Zukofsky

Elliott Carter

In sleep where all_____ that's past_____ goes_ on—

A dawn loves_ more than sleep._____ Clear as leaves of spring._

Loves_____ no less, win - ter- ing,_____ Green - er_____ than_ sum - mer_____ goes–

A sleep_____ gain - says the dawn._____

Nov. 25, 2008 NYC

3. Finally a Valentine

Louis Zukofsky

Elliott Carter

Oct. 15, 2008 NYC

4. O Sleep

Louis Zukofsky

Elliott Carter

Oct. 13, 2008 NYC

5. The Rains

Louis Zukofsky

Elliott Carter

Dec. 23, 2008 NYC

6. Rune

Louis Zukofsky

Elliott Carter

Dec. 23, 2008 NYC

7. Strange

Louis Zukofsky

Elliott Carter

Nov. 26, 2008 NYC

8. Daisy

Louis Zukofsky

Elliott Carter

Nov. 2, 2008 NYC

9. You Who Were Made for This Music

Louis Zukofsky

Elliott Carter

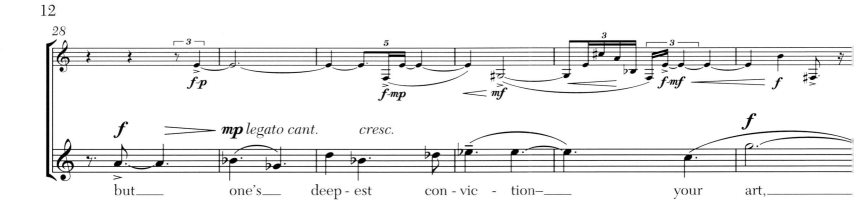

but___ one's___ deep-est con-vic - tion—___ your art,___

___ its___ use—___ you,___ hap-py, by rote,

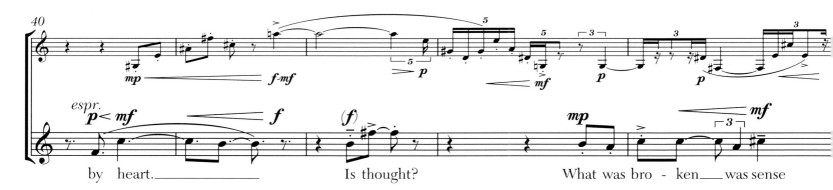

by heart.___ Is thought? What was bro - ken___ was sense

but is hap-py___ a - gain___ al-most seen,___ the first trem-bling of a

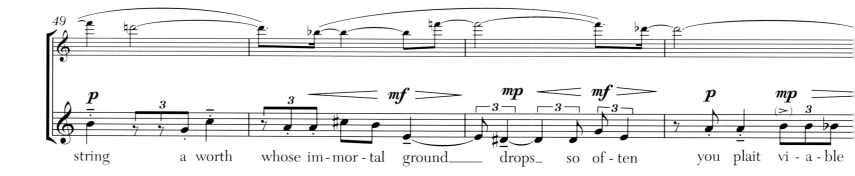

string a worth whose im-mor-tal ground___ drops_ so of-ten you plait vi - a - ble

Oct. 29, 2008 NYC